PIANO • VOCAL • GUITAR

10,000 REASONS
MATT REDMAN

ISBN 978-1-4584-1186-0

HAL•LEONARD®
CORPORATION

7777 W. BLUEMOUND RD. P.O. BOX 13819 MILWAUKEE, WI 53213

Visit Hal Leonard Online at
www.halleonard.com

We Are the Free

Words and Music by JONAS MYRIN
and MATT REDMAN

Capo 3 (G)

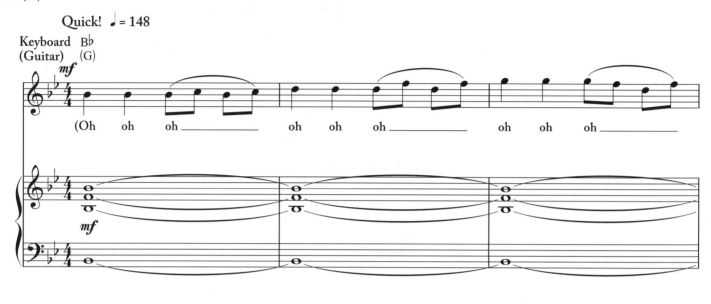

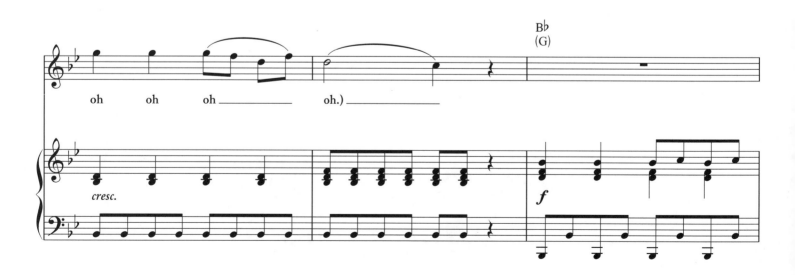

Chords Used in This Song

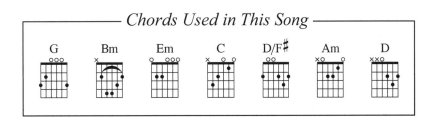

Here for You

Words and Music by TIMOTHY WANSTALL,
MATT REDMAN, MATT MAHER
and JESSE REEVES

Anthemic ♩ = 85

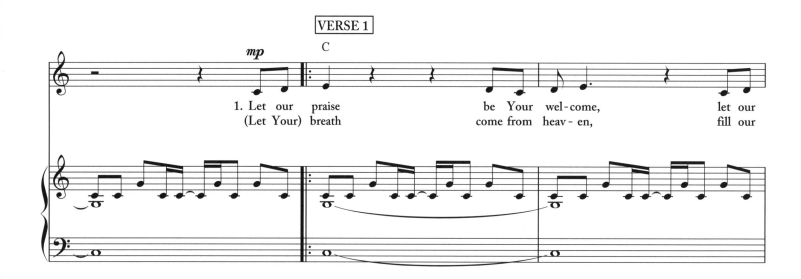

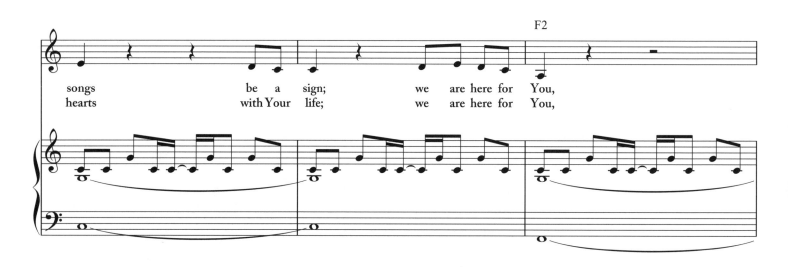

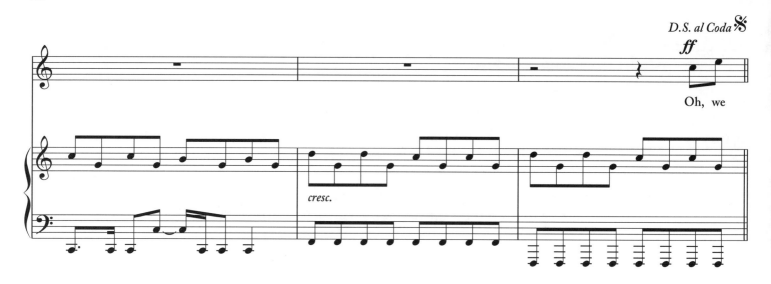

Chords Used in This Song

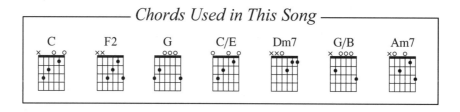

Holy

Words and Music by JASON INGRAM,
MATT REDMAN and JONAS MYRIN

Capo 3 (G)

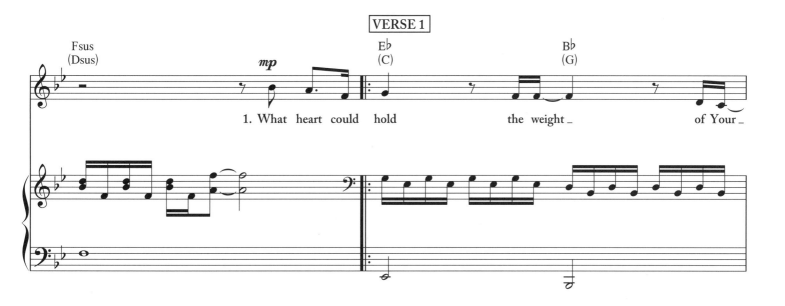

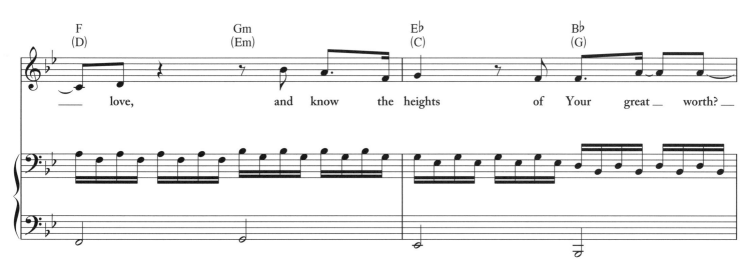

What eyes could look on ____ Your glo-

-ri-ous face, shin-ing like the __ sun? __

1. What heart could ____

2. You are

CHORUS

ho-ly, ho-ly, ho-ly, God most high and God most

shin - ing like the __ sun. _____

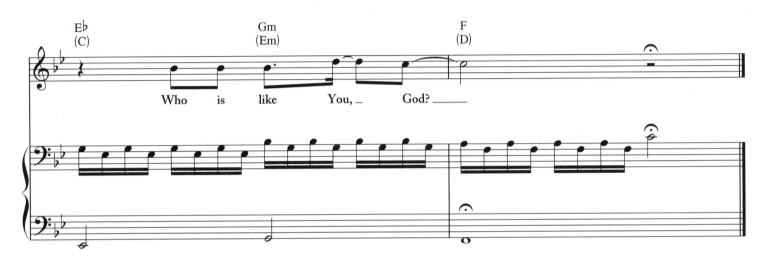

Who is like You, __ God? _____

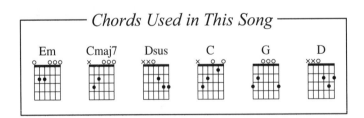

Chords Used in This Song

10,000 Reasons
(Bless the Lord)

Words and Music by JONAS MYRIN
and MATT REDMAN

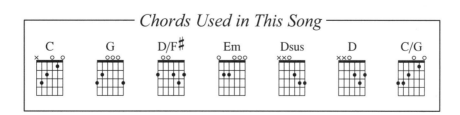

Fires

Words and Music by JONAS MYRIN
and MATT REDMAN

Capo 3 (G)

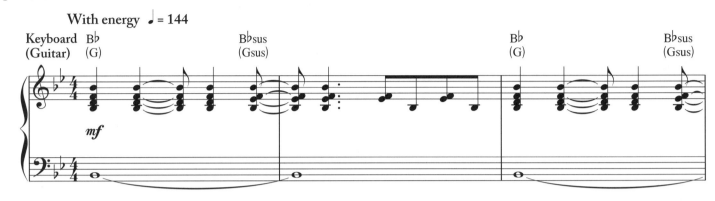

INTRO

You will keep the fires burn-

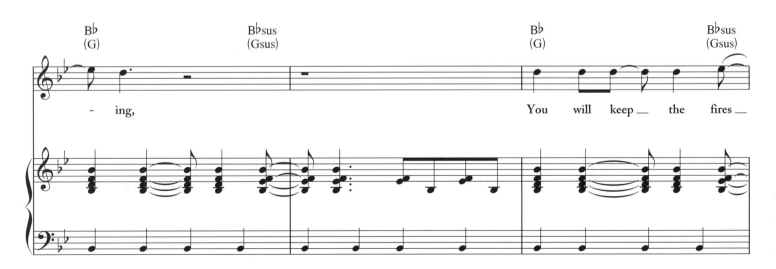

-ing, You will keep the fires

46

OUTRO

You will keep the fires burn - ing,

You will keep the fires burn -

- ing.

Chords Used in This Song

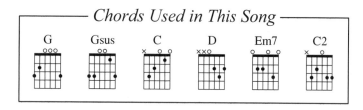

Never Once

Words and Music by JASON INGRAM,
MATT REDMAN and JONAS MYRIN

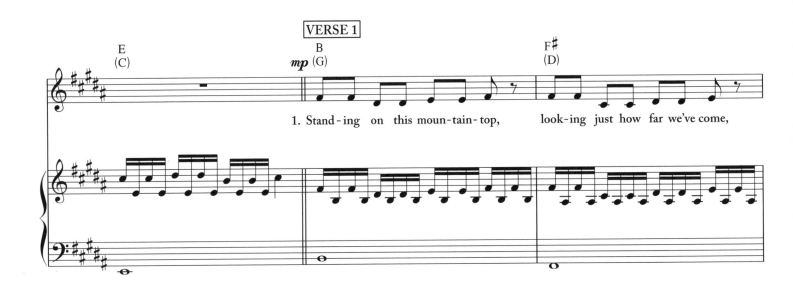

1. Stand-ing on this moun-tain-top, look-ing just how far we've come,

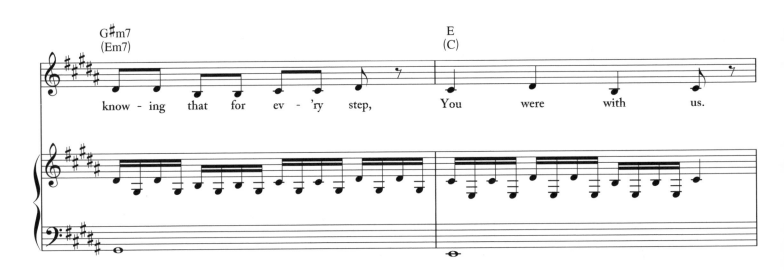

know - ing that for ev -'ry step, You were with us.

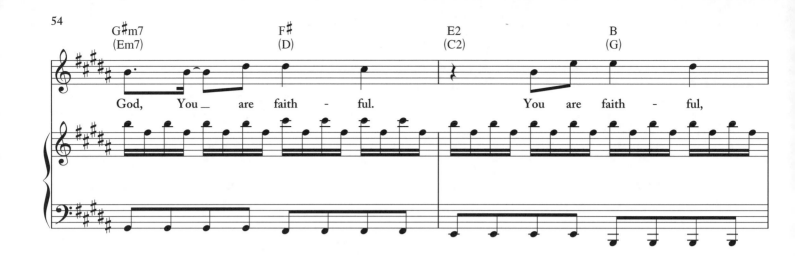

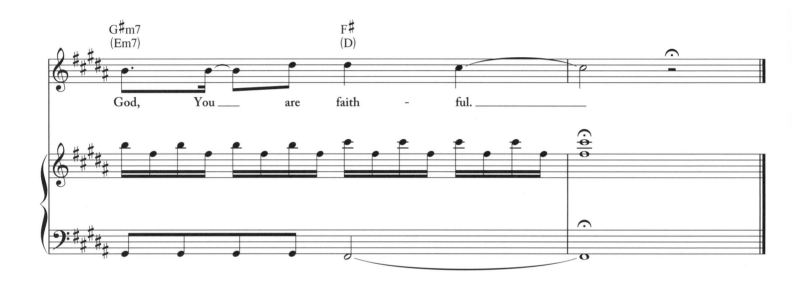

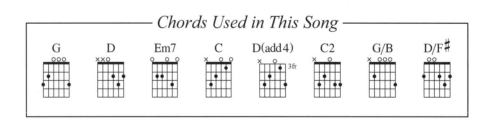

Where Would We Be

Words and Music by JASON INGRAM,
MATT REDMAN and JONAS MYRIN

Capo 4 (G)

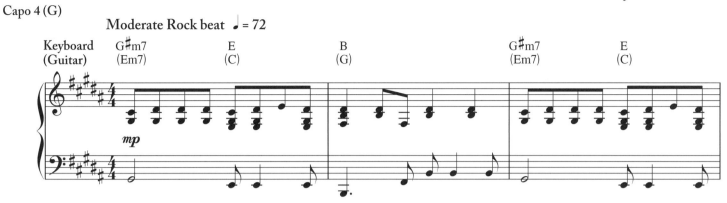

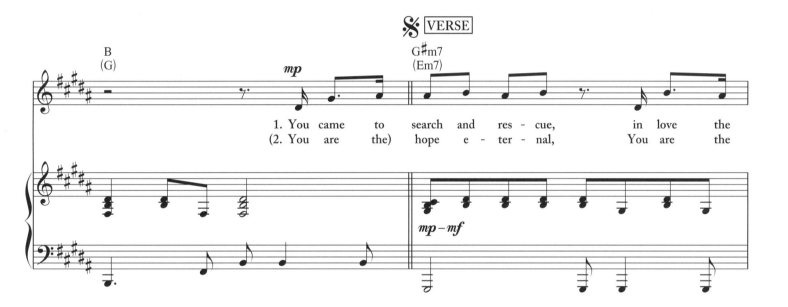

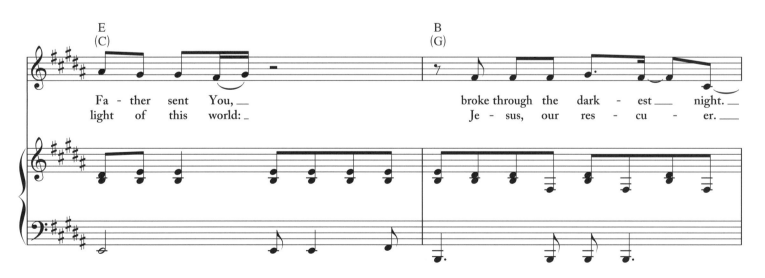

CHORUS 2

62

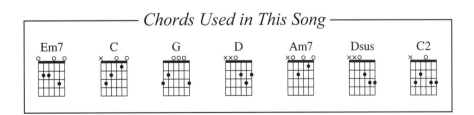

We Could Change the World

Words and Music by JASON INGRAM,
MATT REDMAN and JONAS MYRIN

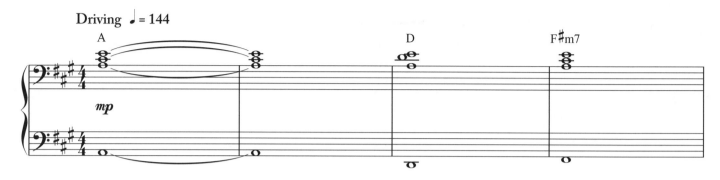

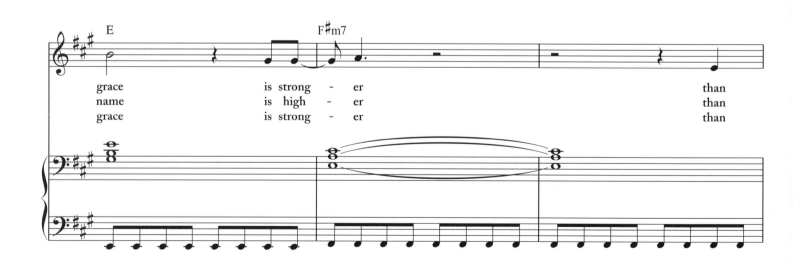

BRIDGE

72

we could change the world. ____ We be - lieve, ____ we be - lieve.

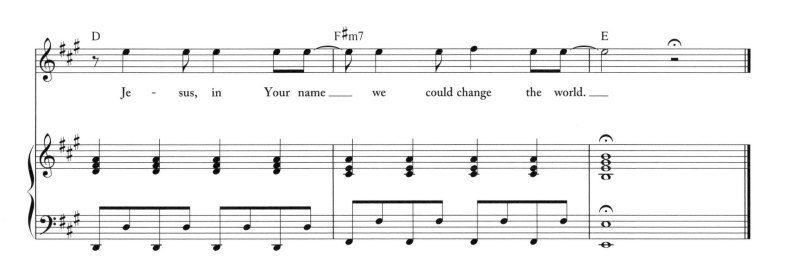

Je - sus, in Your name ____ we could change the world. ____

Chords Used in This Song

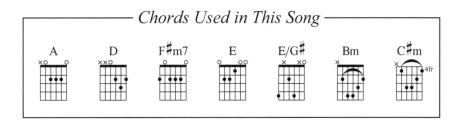

A   D   F#m7   E   E/G#   Bm   C#m

Magnificent

Words and Music by JONAS MYRIN
and MATT REDMAN

Capo 1 (E)

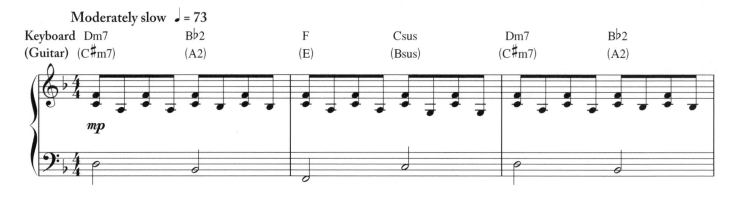

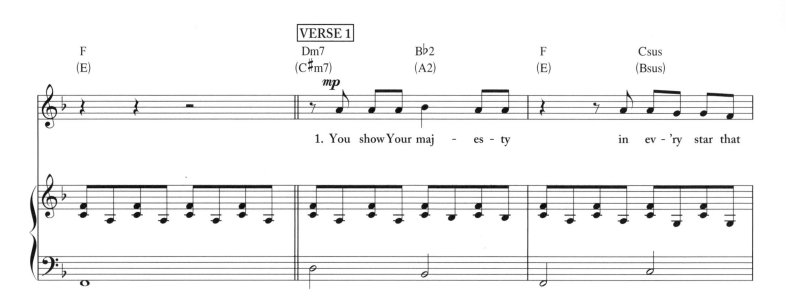

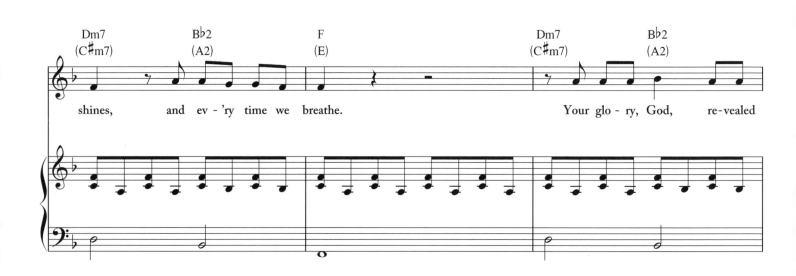

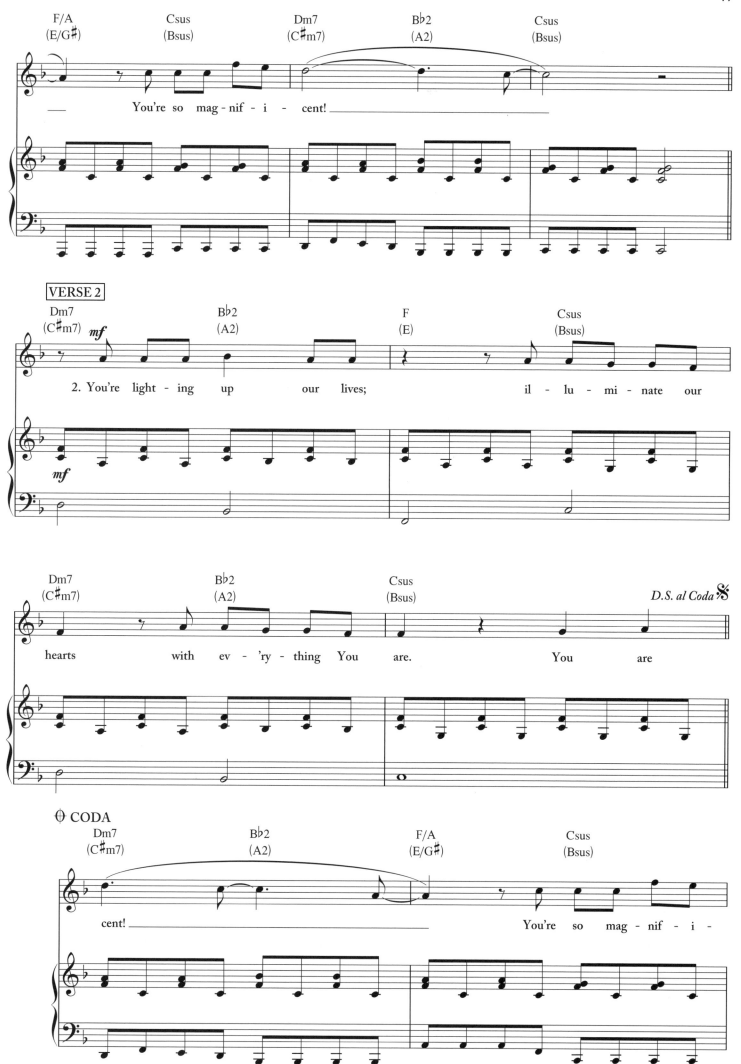

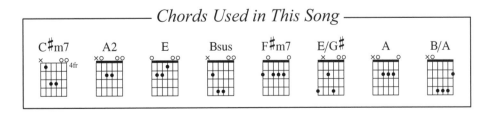

Chords Used in This Song

O This God

Words and Music by JONAS MYRIN
and MATT REDMAN

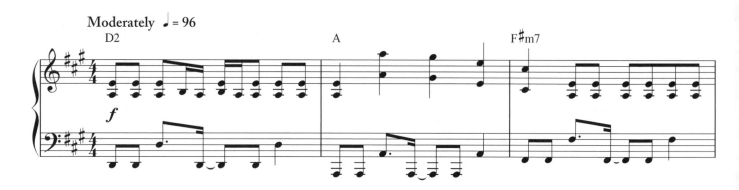

We won't take our eyes off __ You. __ Je - sus, You'll for - ev - er be the __

__ One. We'll have no oth - er God but __ You. __

1.
Je - sus, __

2.

Chords Used in This Song

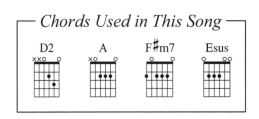

D2   A   F♯m7   Esus

Endless Hallelujah

Words and Music by JONAS MYRIN,
CHRIS TOMLIN and TIM WANSTALL

Capo 1 (G)

ev - 'ry - thing___ as it___ was meant__ to be.___ And we will
ev - 'ry - thing___ I am___ be - fore___ Your throne.___

CHORUS

wor - ship, wor - ship; for - ev - er in___ Your pres - ence we will

sing. We will wor - ship, wor - ship You,___ an

end - less hal - le - lu - jah to the King.___

BRIDGE

No more _____ tears, no more _____ shame, no more sin and sor - row ev - er known _ a - gain. _____ No more _____ fears, no more _____ pain; we will see You face _ to face, _

92

CHORUS

And we will wor - ship,

wor - ship; for - ev - er in ___ Your pres - ence we will

sing, we will sing! We will wor - ship,

wor - ship You, ___ an end - less hal - le - lu - jah to the King, ___

an end-less hal - le - lu - jah to the King.

We'll sing an end-less hal - le - lu - jah to the King.

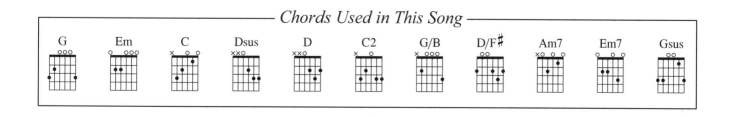

Chords Used in This Song

G   Em   C   Dsus   D   C2   G/B   D/F#   Am7   Em7   Gsus